MEDITERRANEAN DIET
Made Easy

*A Simple Cookbook for Two with 100+ Heart-Healthy
Recipes for Weight Loss. Includes 30-Day Meal Plan
and Shopping Lists*

ABOUT THE AUTHOR

Madeleine Pan, 42, was born and grew up in Palavas-les-Flots, a fishing village near Montpellier in the south of France on the Mediterranean coast. She spent her teenage summers working in the kitchens of the local bistros in the area. As a young adult, she went on to a world-renowned culinary school in Paris, and worked in several award-winning restaurants in France, Italy, and Spain.

After emigrating to Louisiana in the US in her thirties, she was surprised to discover how many Americans thought the food of her native Mediterranean culture was difficult to make for themselves, thinking it was refined, elevated, "cheffy" food that could only be created by professionals in a restaurant.

It's just not true," she explains. "At home, we have always been proud of how simple our food is. We have good ingredients and do as little to them as possible, to let their flavors shine."

"She was also confused by how many people thought that healthy eating was similarly complicated. She enrolled on a nutrition course, but found that everything taught on it was just the normal attitudes towards cooking and food with which she and her European peers had grown up.

"It is crazy to me how Americans are told by the diet industry that they will only be healthy if they buy these expensive diet plans or processed products," she says. "Making good, nourishing food is so easy!"

As well as being delicious, Mediterranean food is of course also famously healthy, with heart-healthy olive oils, a focus on fresh fruit and vegetables, fish and seafood, nuts, seeds, whole grains, and fermented dairy products; with meat, butter, and cream used more sparingly, and in smaller portion sizes.

Madeleine is on a mission to help people reconnect with an honest appetite for real food, simply prepared, in sensible portion sizes. "There are no secrets to it," she laughs. "Americans are just as capable of cooking Mediterranean food as we French are, I want to help them understand how easy and tasty it is – and how much they'll feel the health benefits."

COPYRIGHT INFORMATION

here's what's inside

TABLE OF CONTENTS

TABLE OF CONTENTS

INTRODUCTION

Every civilization has its own cultural values, agriculture and cuisines. These cuisines have evolved and are modified over time according to the taste preferences of the populations, food cultivation, and innovations. The Mediterranean Diet is a cultural diet that has been followed for centuries in nations bordering the Mediterranean Sea, including southern France, Greece, Italy, and Spain. This traditional cuisine has gained worldwide attention for its health benefits, especially its role in improving heart health, weight management, and a longer lifespan, as modern health trends increasingly stress longevity and illness prevention (1). These health benefits are gained because this diet comprises complex carbohydrates, low-fat protein, vegetables, fruits and good fats.

The Mediterranean diet is among the best diets in the world and promotes health. Currently, most people are more inclined towards the Western diet, which includes fatty food made from fried red meat. Besides, there is an extra inclusion of cheese, and there is more use of complex carbohydrates (refined wheat products). Along with this, sweets and beverages are also very prevalent. Lifestyle, fast-paced life, and urbanization all influence these dietary habits. People have lost their precious connection with nature, due to which their body responds negatively and gets affected by hypertension, diabetes, heart problems, muscle weakness and mental health problems.

All these issues are caused by poor dietary intake and the lack of essential vitamins and minerals that support health. For example, the Mediterranean lifestyle encourages you to be connected with nature. People from the past had more exposure to the sun, and they didn't suffer from vitamin D deficiency. Moreover, they also used to spend quality time with family, which prevented them from having mental health problems like depression. Deep breathing in fresh air expels the negative energies from the body. Besides this, exercise, a healthy relationship with the spouse, and quality time while eating can stimulate the release of endorphins. These endorphins can calm down stress and anxiety (2).

The chapters of this book will deeply explain the history, key facets and benefits of the Mediterranean diet. Moreover, it will also provide a practical guide to get started with this diet by making nutritious and delicious recipes.

This chapter will cover transforming the Mediterranean diet from simple to broad-spectrum.

THE HISTORICAL PERSPECTIVE

Initially, the Mediterranean diet had diverse options but was not very nutrient-rich. It mainly focused on the foods organically produced around the Mediterranean shores. The diet only had three components: wine, bread, and olive oil. These foods were grown over a long time in the region and served along with legumes and cheese produced from the milk of goats or sheep. The meat was consumed on special occasions. The eating habits of the Greeks also influenced the diet.

Then, a bit of revolution emerged during the reign of the Roman Empire (400 to 800AD). The Barbarian population introduced the tradition of eating uncultivated food products like meat. Meat from pigs and game animals was consumed. Game animals are wild animals not grown domestically, like deer, bison, rabbits, pigeons, wild boars, quail, etc. The barbarian population also lighted up the trend of eating vegetables. During this tenure, the previous concept of the Mediterranean diet's wheat-olive oil-wine triad was converted into meat-lard-beer.

In the 19th Century, the trend shifted towards carbohydrate intake. The Arabs brought this evolution to Italy. They promoted carbohydrate intake in the form of dried pasta and rice and introduced the use of various seasonings and condiments.

After discovering Americana, multiple new foods were added to the Mediterranean diet. These foods mainly included turkey, corn, tomatoes, beans, potatoes, pineapples, strawberries, peanuts, coconut, sugar, coffee and chocolate. They were also the trendsetters in consuming newly fangled vegetables like eggplants, artichokes, spinach, limes, and lemons. Besides, they added flavours into the diet in the form of ginger, nutmeg, cloves, cinnamon, and saffron (3).

EVOLUTION OF THE MEDITERRANEAN DIET

You can view the table given below about the history of the Mediterranean diet and how it has evolved:

Time	Historical event	Influence on the Mediterranean Diet
Ancient Times	Greek and Roman Civilizations	A triad of bread, olives, and wine was introduced.
4th Century BC	Greek physician Hippocrates	Hippocrates highlighted the benefits of the natural diet and termed it medicine.
Roman Empire (400 to 800AD)	Expansion of the Roman Empire across the Mediterranean	Wheat, olives and legumes were widely cultivated across the Mediterranean basin
Middle Ages (5th – 15th Century))	Arab influences, especially in Spain and Sicily	The trend of eating carbohydrates began in the form of pasta and rice. Also, seasonings and condiments gained popularity.
16th Century	Age of Exploration & Columbian Exchange	New American ingredients, such as tomatoes, potatoes, and peppers, were introduced.
19th Century	Industrial revolution	Development in the field of food processing progressed.
1940s – 1950s	Research by Ancel Keys	Ancel Keys conducted an exploratory study in Greece, Italy, Spain, South Africa, Japan, and Finland to examine the connection between dietary patterns and heart disease. His analysis declared the Mediterranean diet a cardioprotective diet (4).
1960s	Popularization of the Mediterranean Diet	Keys' research highlighted the health benefits of the Mediterranean Diet
1990s – Present	Immense research was performed on the benefits of the Mediterranean diet.	Researchers emphasized the critical benefits of including plant-based foods, olive oil, and lean proteins in the diet.

We will briefly discuss research on the potential benefits of the Mediterranean diet and will unravel the mechanism of action of foods that do this marvellous job.

The Mediterranean Diet's scientific foundation is robust, with countless studies highlighting its benefits for heart health, weight management, brain function, and longevity. Its combination of nutrient-rich foods, healthy fats, and antioxidants, along with its emphasis on moderation and enjoyment of food, makes it one of the most influential and sustainable dietary patterns available today.

WHAT IS THE MEDITERRANEAN DIET

The Mediterranean word's literal meaning is "sea in the middle of the land". When we imagine a sea region, we see water on one side of the picture and, on the other side, long trees of vegetables and fruits, primarily olives, bananas, coconuts, etc. Countries located in this coastal region are closer to nature. People living in this region opt for readily available and freshly harvested foods.

SEAFOOD

People residing around the Mediterranean basin are blessed with fresh fish and seafood. Seafood is long hailed for its nutritional value and exceptional vital vitamins and minerals content. It has many health benefits and can lower the risk of heart issues. It contains an ample amount of vitamin A, thus supporting vision. It is packed with other essential nutrients and vitamins for fetal development. It is recommended that pregnant women aim for 3-4 servings of seafood per week (5).

You will be surprised to know that it can also prevent depression and anxiety. Vitamin D has few food sources, and fatty fish is among the richest. Fatty fish sources include salmon, tuna, anchovy, herring, etc.

NUTS

Nuts and seeds are regular sources of healthy fats and plant-based protein. These are very beneficial for heart health and brain activity.

FRUITS AND VEGETABLES

The Mediterranean diet focuses on consuming fresh seasonal fruits that are not canned by sugar and preservatives.

WHOLE GRAINS

Whole grains provide sustaining energy and don't induce obesity. Bread, pasta, and cereals from whole grains such as wheat and barley are excellent sources.

LEAN PROTEIN

Consumption of red meat is very limited in this diet. The trend is to fulfil protein requirements from plant-based sources like beans, lentils and chickpeas.

MODERATE CONSUMPTION OF DAIRY

Cheese and yoghurt are eaten, often in moderation.

FOOD PYRAMID OF THE MEDITERRANEAN DIET

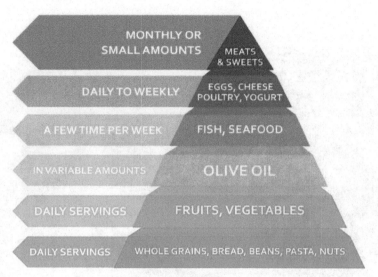

For serving precision, follow the given table (6):

Food groups	Servings
Fruits	2-3 servings/day
Vegetables	5 servings/day
Starchy vegetable (potato)	2-3 times/week
Nuts and seeds	2 times/daily 1 serving 1 ounce/30g
Legumes and beans	2 times/week 1 serving=1/2cup cooked legumes and beans
Poultry, fish, seafood	2 times/week
Eggs	4 whole eggs/week
Red meat	1-2 times/month
Dairy	2 servings/daily
Oils*	Daily use
Vinegar**	Daily use

*Extra virgin olive oil and avocado oil are recommended.
**The Mediterranean diet encourages the addition of vinegar to the diet. These can be balsamic, apple cider, white wine, and vinegar.

PROMINENT HEALTH BENEFITS OF THE MEDITERRANEAN DIET

HEART HEALTH AND CARDIOVASCULAR DISEASE

I think it is everyone's life goal to protect their heart for a healthy and longer lifespan. Otherwise, it becomes difficult for a person to live life to the fullest. Heart patients can't do any physical exertion; otherwise, they may have difficulty breathing. Also, building up of plaque inside the arteries leads to atherosclerosis. Plaque mainly consists of cholesterol that can cause hardening and thickening of arteries. It leads to cardiac arrest and death.

The purpose of telling this short story was to make you understand the cardioprotective role of the Mediterranean diet. It is low in cholesterol, high in good fats, and rich in antioxidants.

OLIVE OIL

Remember the history of the Mediterranean diet! Olive oil was one of the pillars of the triad (wheat-wine-olive oil). It shows that olives are a very nutritious food. Oleuropein is the active component of the olives. It is a glycoside (a form of sugar) that gives a slightly bitter flavour to the olives. It enhances blood flow in arteries through vasodilation and prevents the formation of unnecessary platelets. It also fights with inflammation and oxidative stress (7).

OMEGA-3 FATTY ACIDS

Fats in red meat can raise cholesterol levels, LDL (low-density lipoproteins), and Triglyceride levels. However, the Mediterranean diet depends on food sources containing omega-3 fatty acids. The primary omega-3 fatty acids are EPA (Ecosapentanoic Acid) and DHA (Docosahexanoic Acid) (8). EPA and DHA can prevent the risk of ischemic heart disease and myocardial infarction since these two are modulators of heart rate and blood pressure. It is because of their anti-inflammatory property (9).

IMPACT ON WEIGHT MANAGEMENT AND METABOLIC HEALTH

The Mediterranean Diet is not typically viewed as a restrictive "weight loss" diet but as a sustainable, long-term way of eating. The diet's focus on whole, fibre-rich foods like vegetables, legumes, and whole grains promotes feelings of fullness and reduces the likelihood of overeating. It can help with weight management without the need for strict calorie counting. The healthy fats from olive oil and nuts also contribute to satiety, making it easier to maintain a balanced caloric intake over time.

BRAIN HEALTH AND COGNITIVE FUNCTION

Fish oil has proved to be efficacious in promoting brain development in humans. Moreover, amino acids in salmon can generate multiple neurotransmitters essential for the brain's maintenance. Interminable positive effects of seafood consumption include augmentation of cognitive ability and intelligence.

It is proven through research that a Mediterranean diet can lower the chances of developing Alzheimer's disease (AD) in later life. AD is a brain disorder that slowly destroys memory and thinking skills, eventually making it hard to carry out simple daily tasks. Mediterranean diet is rich in vitamin E, B vitamins, and omega-3 fatty acids, the top-notch nutrients for preventing AD (10).

MIND Diet

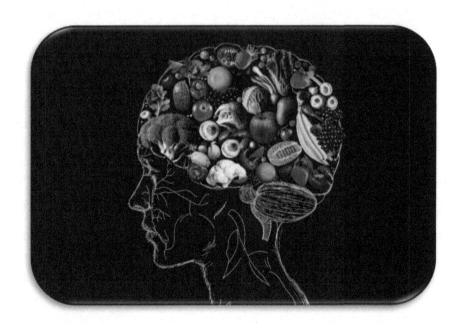

Another fantastic fact about the Mediterranean diet is that it encompasses all the foods categorized as brain foods. MIND Diet combines the Mediterranean diet and DASH (Dietary Approaches to Stop Hypertension), boosting brain performance exponentially. It includes the following foods, according to Harvard School (11).

MIND diet foods for Brain Health	Main role-playing nutrient	Intake recommendation
Green leafy vegetables	B vitamins and vitamin K	6+ servings in a day
Nuts	Omega-3 fatty acids and magnesium	5+ servings in a week
Berries	Antioxidants	2+ servings in a week
Whole grains	B vitamins	3+ servings in a day
Fish	EPA and DHA	
Olive oil	Oleuropein (Neuroprotective component)	Moderate use for meals and seasonings preparation.
Vegetables other than green ones	B vitamins	1+ servings in a week
Poultry	Lean protein	2+ servings in a week
Wine		Not recommended. The wine was added to the initial MIND diet food list. Its moderate intake was linked to cognitive health. However, it is now omitted from the diet for safety reasons.

Mediterranean lifestyle is a calm and joyful way of living that doesn't push you in a daily race where everything passes by, and you can't cherish small moments. Slow mornings and the preparation of breakfast without any hurry are a luxury. This luxury can be understood by only those who prepare their breakfast while their eyes are glued to the ticking clock, and they take the ultra-processed food from the refrigerator and warm it. There is a pleasure in enjoying the aroma of brewed coffee and freshly baked bread. These natural aromas can lighten your mood and induce positive energy to kickstart the day.

A Mediterranean lifestyle is a holistic approach to living that signifies the importance of mind, body and soul. Members from the Mediterranean Lifestyle Institute in Greece postulated a comprehensive definition of this lifestyle, which was later approved as accurate in the Mediterranean Lifestyle Medicine Conference in 2023 (12). The critical facets of the definition included improved health and life longevity, social connectedness and connectivity, community and family values, connection with nature, spirituality and religious practices, diversity and adaptability, and purposeful life.

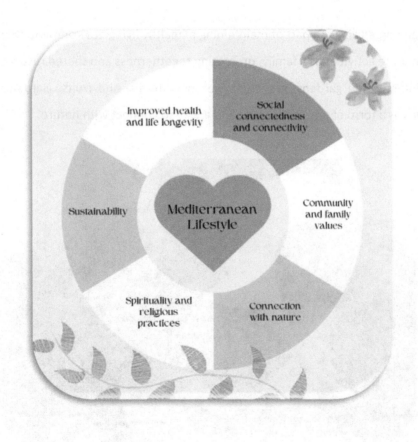

PROMISES HEALTH AND LONGEVITY OF LIFE

Everyone wants to live a healthy life and protect their physical and mental well-being at any cost. Humans also strive to live a long life that is free of health problems like hypertension, diabetes, obesity and cardiac problems. All these problems are set aside when a person starts eating a Mediterranean diet and makes it a lifestyle. Diverging from this lifestyle will only call out problems. A good diet and physical activity attain health and youthfulness. The previous chapters discussed the science behind the Mediterranean diet and its benefits. Now, let's see how this lifestyle incorporates physical activity. A fun fact is that you don't have to buy an expensive membership to the gym. Instead, it would help if you started doing your home chores by yourself. At least you can give it a try!

Here are the traditional house tasks done by people since ages that kept them fit as fiddle:

HOUSEHOLD ACTIVITIES

Regular cleaning and organizing are part of maintaining a healthy living environment. Many Mediterranean cultures engage in these activities as a family, promoting togetherness and shared responsibility. Moreover, women also maintain home gardens, growing vegetables, herbs, and fruits. Gardening provides fresh produce and serves as a form of physical activity and a way to connect with nature.

SOCIAL CONNECTEDNESS AND CONNECTIVITY

Regularly visiting or spending time with neighbours and friends fosters a sense of community. These interactions often occur in communal spaces or during shared meals. Another great tip is to engage in activities like playing games, enjoying music, or dancing together, which is common, especially during celebrations or family gatherings.

CONNECTION WITH NATURE

Connection with nature is essential for releasing the stress from life. You can sense that your soul feels revitalized whenever you visit a beach and watch the sunset. In the present times, it is not necessary to go to the beach every day to relish these moments. You can watch the sunset or gaze at the gleaming light of the moon through your room's window. Besides this, you can enjoy your meals outdoors on a terrace, balcony or garden. This practice fosters a connection with nature and enhances the dining experience.

Remember, while connecting to nature, don't forget to praise the beauty of the universe!

FIX YOUR SLEEP TIMINGS

Also, maintain your sleep schedule according to the time of sunrise and sunset. It keeps your circadian cycle on track and doesn't disturb your hormones. Sleeping late can halt children's growth and imbalance hormones in adults.

Besides a peaceful night's sleep, try to nap midday from 3 pm to 5 pm. Midday naps were commonly valued for promoting physical and mental well-being in ancient Greece. This practice likely originated from the need to avoid the midday heat and conserve energy.

SPIRITUALITY AND RELIGIOUS PRACTICES

A spiritual personality is a goodness attracter! Spirituality can be attained by praying to God daily. Besides this, doing yoga, meditation and practising gratitude creates an intense positive energy and an aura. It protects your mental health and doesn't let the person get depressed.

SUSTAINABILITY

The Mediterranean lifestyle emphasizes sustainability by focusing on seasonal eating, minimizing waste, and sourcing local ingredients. Supporting local farmers reduces the carbon footprint and promotes biodiversity. Leftovers are repurposed, and every part of an ingredient is used, reflecting respect for food and resources. This approach encourages harmony with the environment and responsible living. People genuinely connected to nature know the worth of the food cultivated by so much effort.

The Mediterranean diet is not complex and doesn't require special knowledge or guidance. It is also budget-friendly and easily accessible. Many other diets make you follow strict rules, and even grocery shopping feels like finding a needle in the haystack. For instance, Irritable bowel syndrome patients suffer a lot in finding their favourite snacks that are gluten and lactose-free. This diet ensures a healthy life and can work as a therapeutic diet for hypertension and cardiac patients. It can also be used to maintain an ideal weight.

BE MINDFUL OF YOUR MACROS

While starting the Mediterranean diet, bring yourself back to the old times. You should eat less processed foods and eat organically grown vegetables and fruits. Our meals have three main components: carbohydrates, protein, and fats. These are known as macronutrients/macros. You have to choose these three main things wisely!

Beginning with carbohydrates, use whole grain products that contain enough fibre. These are slowly digested and don't cause a spike in sugar levels. Diabetic patients are also advised to use grains that have bran parts.

Then there comes protein. You should avoid ultra-processed meat products and red meat on the Mediterranean diet. It might be a bit daring for you to avoid beef burgers and steaks. But you can enjoy 2-3 times in a month. Instead, you should try to find delicious and palatable fish. If you're not used to eating fish regularly, start incorporating it into your diet once or twice a week. Grilled or baked fish with a drizzle of olive oil, lemon, and herbs can be a delicious addition to your weekly meals. You can try out the recipes in this book. I am sure your tastebuds will surely love the juiciness and tenderness of fish.

MACRONUTRIENTS

CARBS

PROTEINS

FATS

Lastly, you need to watch out for the kinds of fats you incorporate into your diet. Fats in oil and butter are usually used to prepare meals. You should swap butter for olive oil and make a creamy spread from avocado to replace mayonnaise. Limit unnecessary oil and fulfil your daily fat requirement through good fats. These fats will not wreak havoc on your cholesterol level. But these will protect your heart. Its sources include nuts and seeds. Add them to your meals and snacks.

PLAN YOUR MEALS

Meal planning is a key to success with the Mediterranean Diet. Think about incorporating plant-based foods, lean proteins, and healthy fats into each meal. Do your grocery shopping mindfully. If you bring all the right ingredients, you can come up with anything unique and tasty. For example, make a simple salad with olive oil and lemon dressing, or try a grain bowl with quinoa, vegetables, and grilled fish.

COOK AT HOME

One of the best ways to embrace the Mediterranean Diet is by preparing meals at home. Cooking allows you to control the ingredients and experiment with new flavours. Start by exploring the Mediterranean recipes in this book. Try out one recipe in a day. After the recipe trial period, you will access your food preferences. Then you can keep those repeat those recipes as your comfort food.

SHOP LOCAL

The trend of shopping from local vendors and food stalls is ending over time. They sell freshly harvested food, which is more nutritious than the few days-old food in the marts. You can get the quality products through these stalls at a reasonable price. It also promotes the economic growth of the local people and supports community growth.

SNACK SMART

I know most of you are fond of eating packaged foods. But remember, if you aim to be on the Mediterranean diet, you must be close to nature. It means you should eat things in their natural form. Replace eating packaged potato chips with homemade potato wedges. Besides this, you can savour your favourite seasonal fruit with a small handful of almonds at snack time. This snack will be both satisfying and nutritious.

AVOID THESE FOODS

Sugary drinks (soda, sweetened juices), packaged food, refined grains (such as white bread and pasta), and too much red or processed meats are a big no in the Mediterranean diet. Besides these, avoid trans fats, which are included in many packaged and fried snacks, and limit added sugars and refined sugar-rich desserts.

FIND A COMPANY TO ENJOY YOUR MEALS

In Mediterranean cultures, food is enjoyed slowly and often shared with family and friends. Doing this makes your meals enjoyable. Try to recreate this sense of connection at your meals. You can do this by going with your colleagues or friends during lunch and having a good conversation. Also, offer them the opportunity to taste your food.

I hope these strategies will help you change your eating habits and bring a remarkable change in the food items in the pantry. Remember this: the Mediterranean diet is sustainable. It is not hard to follow, and you can relish every bit of it.

HOW TO USE THIS BOOK

SET REALISTIC GOALS

I know you must be very motivated to try this diet today, and I will try to bring an overnight change. But here, the practical advice is that you must take baby steps. Through this, you can see more progress that will last longer, and you will have reduced chances of reverting to your previous lifestyle. Here are some of the goals you can set for yourself initially.

- In the first week, you can aim to start using olive oil in your food.
- In the next week, you can start avoiding red meat products.
- While avoiding red meat, try new fish and lean meat recipes to keep getting enough protein.
- Another goal that you can set is to have your morning tea/coffee on your balcony/terrace over the weekend. Or you can do anything else that can make your eyes shine bright because of the beauty of nature.
- You can also set up a goal to initially limit beverages to only twice a week. Leaving your favourite foods all of a sudden can ignite its intense craving.

MAKE YOUR GROCERY LIST

Pick up the recipes according to your taste preference, then list the ingredients you need to stock up in your pantry. Try to shop for dried items like grains weekly or monthly. Food products with less shelf should be bought after 2 or 3 days.

CHOOSE THE RIGHT RECIPE

- Each recipe in this book has given a quantity of macronutrients. You can balance your daily carbohydrates, protein and facts requirements according to that.
- Also, cross-check the ingredients with the available food in your pantry before making anything. Missing out one or two ingredients can dampen the true essence of the recipe.
- Besides this, plan a meal according to the available time. The preparation time of our recipe is given. You can take advantage of it and can spend your time mindfully.

CHECK THE BOOK INDEXING

This book comes up with an exact and streamlined indexing. By checking the indexing of the recipes, you can land on the precise page and read. The categorization of recipes into dips, sauces, breakfasts, appetizers, soups, salads, etc. is time-saving to find the exact dish.

Mediterranean Recipes

CHAPTER 5: DIPS, SAUCES AND CONDIMENTS

Tzatziki Sauce

Ingredients

- 1 cup of Greek yogurt
- 1 grated cucumber
- 2 minced garlic cloves
- 1 tablespoon of olive oil
- 1 tablespoon freshly chopped dill
- 1 tablespoon lemon juice
- Salt and pepper

Time: 10

Servings: 4

Calories: 50 Kcal

Instructions

1. Grate cucumber and squeeze its water in a cheesecloth.
2. Mix minced garlic, olive oil, and lemon juice.
3. Then combine it with Greek yogurt, black pepper, salt, and chopped dill.

Hummus

Instructions

- 1 can (15 oz) of rinsed and drained chickpeas
- 2 tablespoons of tahini
- 1 garlic clove
- 2 tablespoons of olive oil
- Half lemon juice
- Water
- Salt as per your taste

Time: 10

Servings: 6

Calories: 80 Kcal

Instructions

1. Put chickpeas, garlic, lemon juice, olive oil, and tahini in a blender.
2. Blend it at high speed until the mixture becomes very creamy and velvety.
3. Add water to get the desired consistency.
4. Drizzle some olive oil over and serve.

Baba Ganoush

Ingredients

- 1 large-sized eggplant
- 1 tablespoon of lemon juice
- 1tablespoon of olive oil
- 2 tablespoons of tahini
- 1 minced garlic clove
- Salt as per your taste

Time: 50

Servings: 4

Calories: 60 Kcal

Instructions

1. Preheat oven to 400°F (200°C). Prick eggplant and roast for 30-40 minutes until soft.
2. Scoop out the flesh of the eggplant and mix it in a food processor with tahini, garlic, lemon juice, and olive oil.

3. Add salt and black pepper to enhance its flavour.
4. Serve it chilled.

Skordalia

Instructions

- 2 medium-sized potatoes peeled
- 1/4 cup of olive oil
- 4 garlic cloves
- 1 tablespoon red wine vinegar
- Salt as per your taste

Time: 25

Servings: 4

Calories: 70 Kcal

Instructions

1. Add the garlic and potatoes and mash until smooth.
2. Then, gradually pour vinegar and olive oil while mixing until the texture becomes smooth.
3. Put on some salt and then serve.

Muhammara

Ingredients

Time: 10   Servings: 4   Calories: 90 Kcal

- Two red bell peppers
- 1 tablespoon pomegranate molasses
- 1 tablespoon of olive oil
- ½ cup of walnuts
- 1 garlic clove
- Salt as per your taste

Instructions

1. Put red peppers, garlic, walnuts, and pomegranate molasses in a food blender.
2. Blend it well, and then add salt.
3. Drizzle olive oil on it and then serve.

CHAPTER 6: BREAKFASTS

Shakshuka

Ingredients

- 1 tablespoon of olive oil
- 4 eggs
- 1½ teaspoon of chilli powder
- 2 large chopped tomatoes
- 1 teaspoon of ground cumin
- 1 teaspoon of paprika
- 1 chopped onion
- 1 sliced red bell pepper
- 2 garlic cloves

Time: 25

Servings: 4

Calories: 160 Kcal

Instructions

1. Take a frying pan. Add olive oil and sauté onion, bell pepper, and garlic. Cook until these ingredients become soft.
2. Add on the spices.
3. Put finely chopped tomatoes in it and simmer it for 5-7mins.
4. When the sauce is ready, crack eggs on it and let it cook in steam for 2-3 min.
5. Garnish it with parsley and serve.

Avocado toast with feta

Instructions

- 1 whole-grain bread slice
- 1/2 a cup of cherry tomatoes
- 1 tablespoon of crumbled feta cheese
- 1/2 an avocado, mashed
- Salt and pepper as per your taste
- Chopped fresh basil

Time: 10

Servings: 1

Calories: 200 Kcal

Instructions

1. Mash avocado in a bowl.
2. Toast a slice of bread.
3. Now spread the avocado over it. Top it with feta cheese and cherry tomatoes.
4. Season it with basil, salt and pepper.

Egg Sandwiches

Ingredients

- 2 pieces of toasted whole-grain bread
- 2 tablespoons of shredded feta cheese
- 2-3 tomato slices
- 1 egg
- 1/4 tsp freshly chopped rosemary
- 1/2 teaspoon of olive oil
- Salt and pepper as per your taste

Time: 15

Servings: 1

KCAL

Calories: 220 Kcal

Instructions

1. Whisk the egg, salt, pepper, and rosemary together in a small bowl.
2. Take a frying pan. Add olive in it and then oil mixture and scramble it until cooked.
3. Spread the scrambled egg on one slice of bread. Top it with feta and tomato slices.
4. Cover it with the other toasted slice of bread and serve it warm.

Halloumi and Tomato Stack

Instructions

- 1 sliced tomato
- 3 slices of halloumi cheese
- 1 tsp olive oil
- Fresh basil

Time: 10

Servings: 1

KCAL

Calories: 220 Kcal

Instructions

1. Grill halloumi slices till they turn out golden.
2. Layer halloumi and tomato slices on top of each other.
3. Drizzle some olive on it and garnish it with basil leaves.

Berry-Almond Smoothie Bowl

Ingredients

- 1 cup mixed berries
- ½ sliced banana
- 1/4th cup granola
- 1 tablespoon of almonds
- 1/2 cup almond milk

 Time: 5

 Servings: 1

 Calories: 250 Kcal

Instructions

1. Put the banana, mixed berries, and almond milk in a blender. Blend until it's smooth.
2. In a bowl, pour the smoothie.
3. If preferred, garnish with fresh berries, granola, and sliced almonds.
4. Serve it right away.

Mediterranean Frittata

Instructions

- 1 tablespoon of olive oil
- 4 large eggs
- 1/2 red bell pepper
- 1/2 cup of cherry tomatoes
- 1/2 onion
- 1/2 a zucchini
- 1/4 cup of feta cheese
- Chopped parsley

 Time: 25

 Servings: 4

 Calories: 170 Kcal

Instructions

1. Turn the oven on to 190°C.
2. In an oven-safe skillet, heat the olive oil and cook the bell pepper, zucchini, and onion.
3. Cook for a further 2 minutes after adding the cherry tomatoes.
4. Add feta cheese to the skillet after whisking eggs with spices.
5. After transferring, bake for 10 to 12 minutes or until the eggs are set. Add parsley as a garnish.

Hummus and Vegetable Wrap

Ingredients

- 1 tortilla made of whole grains
- 3 tablespoons of hummus
- 1/4 sliced cucumber
- 1/4 sliced red bell pepper
- 1/4 sliced avocado
- A handful of spinach leaves

Time: 5

Servings: 1

Calories: 250 Kcal

Instructions

1. Toast the tortilla in a pan. Spread hummus over it.
2. Top it with cucumber, bell pepper, avocado, and spinach.
3. Roll it firmly and enjoy.

Quinoa Bowl

Instructions

- 1/2 cup of cooked quinoa
- 1/4th of a cucumber
- 1/2 a cup of cherry tomatoes
- 1 tablespoon of olive oil
- 2 tablespoons of chopped olives
- 1/4th cup of sliced feta cheese
- Fresh parsley

Time: 25

Servings: 2

Calories: 220 Kcal

Instructions

1. Combine cooked quinoa, tomatoes, cucumber, olives, and feta in a bowl.
2. Drizzle with olive oil and garnish with herbs.

Spinach and Feta Omelette

Ingredients

- 2 eggs
- ½ cup chopped spinach
- 2 tablespoons of crumbled feta cheese
- Salt and pepper as per your taste

Time: 10

Servings: 1

Calories: 150 Kcal

Instructions

1. Beat eggs.
2. Add spinach in it with salt and pepper.
3. Cook the egg mixture in a nonstick frypan until the eggs are set.
4. Fold the omelette in half, add the feta, and cook until the cheese melts.

Egg Muffins

Instructions

- 6 eggs
- 1/4 cup of spinach, chopped
- 1/4 cup of bell peppers, chopped
- 1/4 cup chopped cherry tomatoes
- 1/4 cup of crumbled feta cheese

Time: 30

Servings: 6

Calories: 70 Kcal

Instructions

1. Grease a muffin tray and preheat the oven to 350°F (175°C).
2. Add the spinach, bell pepper, tomatoes, and feta to a bowl with whisked eggs.
3. Fill muffin tins, then bake for 18 to 20 minutes.

CHAPTER 7: APPETIZERS

Marinated Olives

Ingredients

- 1 cup of mixed olives
- 1 tablespoon of lemon zest
- 1 chopped garlic clove
- 1 tablespoon of olive oil
- 1 teaspoon of freshly chopped rosemary

 Time: 5

 Servings: 6

 Calories: 60 Kcal

Instructions

1. Combine olive oil, lemon zest, garlic, and rosemary with the olives.
2. Before serving, let it marinate for at least an hour.

Caprese Skewers

Instructions

- 16 cherry tomatoes
- 16 fresh basil leaves
- 1 tablespoon balsamic glaze
- 16 balls of fresh mozzarella

 Time: 10

 Servings: 8

 Calories: 40 Kcal

Instructions

1. Take skewers and thread them with tomato, basil leaves, and mozzarella balls one by one.
2. Drizzle balsamic glaze on it, and it is ready to serve.

Stuffed Grape Leaves (Dolmas)

Ingredients

 Time: 50

 Servings: 6

 Calories: 50 Kcal

- 20 jarred grape leaves
- 1 cup of cooked rice
- 1 tablespoon of pine nuts
- 1 tablespoon of currants
- 2 tablespoons of lemon juice
- 1 tablespoon of freshly chopped dill

Instructions

1. Thoroughly rinse grapes leaves and lay them flat.
2. Combine rice, lemon juice, dill, pine nuts, and currants.
3. Roll tightly after inserting a teaspoon into each grape leaf.
4. Before serving, let it steam for 20 minutes.

Greek Spinach Pie

Instructions

 Time: 45

 Servings: 6

 Calories: 80 Kcal

- 1 cup of spinach
- 1 minced garlic clove
- 1 egg
- ¼ cup crumbled feta cheese
- 1 chopped spinach
- 6 sheets of phyllo pastry
- Olive oil

Instructions

1. Mix garlic, egg, feta, and spinach in a bowl.
2. Place the filling in the middle of the phyllo sheets after brushing them with oil.
3. Roll up and bake for 20 to 30 minutes at 375°F (190°C).

Falafel Balls

Ingredients

Time: 30

Servings: 8

Calories: 60 Kcal

- 1 can of drained chickpeas
- 1 small onion
- 1 tablespoon of fresh parsley
- 1 teaspoon of cumin powder
- 1 minced garlic clove
- 2 tablespoons of flour
- Salt and pepper as per your taste

Instructions

1. Blend all the ingredients in a food processor until it becomes smooth.
2. Shape them into small balls and then bake them at 190°C for 20 minutes.

Tomato Brochette

Instructions

Time: 15

Servings: 6

Calories: 50 Kcal

- 6 baguette slices
- 1 cup of diced cherry tomatoes
- 1 minced garlic clove
- 1 tablespoon of chopped fresh basil
- Salt and pepper as per your taste

Instructions

1. Toast slices of baguette in a skillet.
2. Add salt, pepper, garlic, basil, and tomatoes.
3. Serve by spooning onto toast.

Greek Cucumber Cups

Ingredients

- 1 large-sized cucumber
- ½ cup of crumbled feta cheese
- 1 tablespoon of freshly chopped dill
- ½ cup of Greek yogurt
- Salt and pepper as per your taste

Time: 15

Servings: 6

Calories: 35 Kcal

Instructions

1. Make little cups of cucumber by hollowing them out in rounds.
2. Combine feta, Greek yogurt, and dill.
3. Transfer it to cucumber cups using a spoon and serve.

Mediterranean Chickpea Salad

Instructions

- 1 can of drained chickpeas
- 1 cup of cherry tomatoes
- 1cup of chopped red onion
- 2 tablespoons of olive oil
- ½ cucumber
- 1 tablespoon of lemon juice
- Salt and pepper as per your taste

Time: 10

Servings: 6

Calories: 60 Kcal

Instructions

1. Combine the red onion, cucumber, tomatoes, and chickpeas in a bowl.
2. Add lemon juice, salt, pepper, and olive oil and toss.

CHAPTER 8: SOUPS

Turkish Red Lentil Soup

Ingredients

- 1 tablespoon of olive oil
- 1 sliced onion
- 1 cup of red lentils
- 4 cups of vegetable broth
- ½ teaspoon of cumin
- ½ teaspoon of paprika
- 1 sliced carrot
- Salt and pepper as per your taste
- Slices of lemon

 Time: 40

 Servings: 4

 Calories: 200 Kcal

Instructions

1. In a pot, heat the olive oil and cook the carrots and onions until they are tender.
2. Add the lentils, broth, paprika, and cumin in a pot. Cover the lid of the pot and let the lentils get boiled.
3. Lentils should be soft after 25 minutes of simmering.
4. Serve it with lemon wedges and season with salt and pepper.

Spanish Gazpacho

Instructions

- 1/4th cup of olive oil
- 6 ripe tomatoes
- 1 slice cucumber
- 1 green bell pepper
- 1 small onion
- 2 chopped garlic cloves
- 2 tablespoons red wine vinegar
- Salt and pepper

 Time: 15

 Servings: 4

 Calories: 150 Kcal

Instructions

1. In a blender, combine all the ingredients until they are smooth.
2. Before serving, chill for two to three hours.
3. Garnish with chopped herbs or veggies and serve chilled.

Italian Minestrone

Ingredients

- 1 tablespoon of olive oil
- 1 chopped onion
- 2 minced garlic cloves
- 1 chopped zucchini
- 15 oz kidney beans
- 15 oz ttomatoes
- 4 cups of vegetable broth
- 2 chopped carrots
- 2 celery stalks
- 1/2 cup macaroni
- 1 tsp of dried basil
- 1 tsp dried oregano

 Time: 55

 Servings: 6

 Calories: 210 Kcal

Instructions

1. In a big pot, heat the olive oil. For around five minutes, sauté the celery, carrots, onion, and garlic until they are tender.
2. Add the broth, tomatoes, beans, and zucchini. Boil the mixture, and then let it simmer.
3. Add pasta and herbs and simmer for 10 to 12 minutes or until pasta is cooked.
4. Add salt and pepper to taste.

Tomato Basil Soup

Instructions

- 1 tablespoon of olive oil
- 1 can (28 ounces) of crushed tomatoes
- 1/4 cup of fresh basil leaves
- 3 cups of vegetable broth
- Salt and pepper as per your taste

 Time: 20

 Servings: 4

 Calories: 90 Kcal

Instructions

1. In a pot, heat the olive oil.
2. Simmer it for ten minutes after adding the tomatoes and broth.
3. Add fresh basil and blend until smooth.
4. Add salt and pepper to taste.

Greek Lemon Chickpea Soup

Ingredients

- 1 tablespoon of olive oil
- 1 can of drained chickpeas
- 4 cups of vegetable broth
- 1 lemon, squeezed
- Garnish with fresh parsley
- Salt and pepper as per your taste

Time: 25

Servings: 4

Calories: 150 Kcal

Instructions

1. In a pot, heat the olive oil, add the chickpeas, and sauté for two minutes.
2. After adding the broth and bringing it to a boil, simmer it for fifteen minutes.
3. Season with salt, pepper, and lemon juice. Add parsley as a garnish.

Italian Ribollita

Instructions

- 1 tablespoon of olive oil
- 1 can (15oz) of white beans
- 1 can (15oz) can of chopped tomatoes
- 2 cups of stale bread chunks
- 4 cups of vegetable broth
- Salt and pepper as per your taste

Time: 25

Servings: 4

Calories: 210 Kcal

Instructions

1. In a big pot, heat the olive oil. Bring the broth, tomatoes, and beans to a boil.
2. Add the bread cubes, simmer, and cook for ten minutes or until the bread is tender.
3. Add salt and pepper for seasoning. If desired, garnish with fresh herbs.

Lebanese Lentil Soup

Ingredients

Time: 45

Servings: 4

Calories: 180 Kcal

- 1 tablespoon of olive oil
- 1 chopped onion
- 2 minced garlic cloves
- 1 cup of washed red lentils
- ½ a cup of optional rice
- 6 cups of veggie broth
- 1 teaspoon of ground cumin
- 1 teaspoon of ground coriander

Instructions

1. Heat the olive oil in a pot and cook the garlic and onion until they are tender.
2. Add rice, broth, lentils, and seasonings. Bring to a boil, then simmer, stirring regularly, for 25 to 30 minutes.
3. Add salt and pepper for seasoning. Garnish with parsley and lemon wedges.

CHAPTER 9: SALADS

Tabbouleh

Ingredients

Time: 15

Servings: 4

Calories: 90 Kcal

- 1 cup of cooked bulgur
- 2 tablespoons lemon juice
- ½ cup chopped fresh parsley and
- ½ cup cherry tomatoes
- Salt as per your taste

Instructions

1. In a bowl, combine cooked bulgur, tomatoes, and parsley.
2. Add salt and lemon juice.
3. Toss all ingredients to mix them uniformly.

Cucumber Yogurt Salad

Instructions

Time: 5

Servings: 4

Calories: 60 Kcal

- 1 thinly sliced cucumber
- 1 cup Greek yogurt
- 1 tablespoon of chopped fresh dill
- Salt and pepper as per your taste

Instructions

1. Add thinly sliced cucumber to a yoghurt bowl.
2. Season it with black pepper and salt.
3. Garnish dill over it for the final look.

Caprese Salad

Ingredients

Time: 5

Servings: 4

Calories: 160 Kcal

- 2 large-sized tomato
- 1 cup fresh mozzarella
- 1 tablespoon of olive oil
- Salt and pepper as per your taste

Instructions

1. On a platter, arrange mozzarella and tomatoes in layers.
2. Season with salt and pepper and drizzle with olive oil.

Olive and Tomato Salad

Instructions

Time: 5

Servings: 4

Calories: 80 Kcal

- 1 tablespoon of olive oil
- 1 cup cherry tomatoes cut into halves
- ½ cup olives cut into halves
- ¼ cup of feta cheese
- Salad leaves
- Salt and pepper as per your taste

Instructions

1. Mix tomatoes, feta cheese, salad leaves, and olives in a bowl.
2. Then drizzle with olive oil and add salt to taste.

Carrot Tahini Salad

Ingredients

- 2 shredded carrots
- 1 tablespoon of lemon juice
- 1 tablespoon of tahini

Time: 5

Servings: 4

Calories: 50 Kcal

Instructions

1. Shred the carrots through a grater. Add lemon juice and tahini to it.
2. Toss it well and serve.

Tomato and Mozzarella Salad

Instructions

- 2 large-sized tomatoes
- ½ mozzarella cheese cubes
- Salt and pepper as per your taste

Time: 5

Servings: 4

Calories: 90 Kcal

Instructions

1. Chop two large tomatoes. Cut mozzarella cheese into cubes.
2. Mix both of the ingredients in a bowl and season it with salt and pepper.

Quick Beet Salad

Ingredients

Time: 5   Servings: 4   Calories: 50 Kcal

- 1 cup canned beets
- 1 tablespoon of olive oil
- Salt and pepper as per your taste
- Coriander for garnishing

Instructions

1. Toss beets with olive oil and spices.
2. Garnish it with coriander, and the simplest salad is ready.

Green Bean Salad

Instructions

Time: 10   Servings: 4   Calories: 90 Kcal

- 1 cup cooked green beans
- 1/4th ricotta cheese
- 2 tablespoons of sliced almonds
- 1 tablespoon of olive oil
- Salt and pepper as per your taste

Instructions

1. Sautee green beans for 5 minutes.
2. Sprinkle shredded ricotta cheese over it.
3. Season it with spices, sprinkle sliced almonds on it, and serve.

CHAPTER 10: VEGETABLES

Hummus and Vegetable Wrap

Ingredients

 Time: 5

 Servings: 1

 Calories: 250 Kcal

- 1 tortilla made of whole grains
- 3 tablespoons of hummus
- 1/4 sliced cucumber
- 1/4 sliced red bell pepper
- 1/4 sliced avocado
- A handful of spinach leaves

Instructions

1. Toast the tortilla in a pan. Spread hummus over it.
2. Top it with cucumber, bell pepper, avocado, and spinach.
3. Roll it firmly and enjoy.

Spanish Grilled Bell Peppers

Instructions

 Time: 20

 Servings: 4

 Calories: 90 Kcal

- 3 large-sized bell peppers
- 2 tablespoons of olive oil
- Salt and pepper as per your taste

Instructions

1. Cut any coloured bell pepper into strips shape. Toss them with salt and pepper.
2. Place it on the grill or in the frying pan.
3. Cook it on low heat for 10-15 min until it gets charred and tender.

Italian Sauteed Zucchini

Ingredients

- 3 zucchinis
- 1 tablespoon of olive oil
- Salt and pepper as per your taste

Time: 15

Servings: 4

Calories: 60 Kcal

Instructions

1. Slice zucchinis and set it aside.
2. Eat olive oil in a skillet and put zucchini in it. Sauté it for 10 minutes until it gets tender and brown.
3. Season it with salt and pepper.

Lebanese Roasted Cauliflower

Instructions

- 1 cauliflower head
- 1 tablespoon of olive oil
- Salt and pepper as per your taste

Time: 30

Servings: 4

Calories: 80 Kcal

Instructions

1. Cut the cauliflower head into florets.
2. Preheat oven to 400°F (200°C). Toss cauliflower florets with olive oil, salt, and pepper.
3. Spread on a baking sheet and roast for 25 minutes until golden and tender.

Moroccan Salad

Ingredients

- 1 sliced zucchini
- 2 large-sized tomatoes
- 2 tablespoons of olive oil
- 1 sliced eggplant
- Salt and pepper as per your taste
- Garnish with fresh thyme

 Time: 9

 Servings: 4

 Calories: 100 Kcal

Instructions

1. Turn the oven on to 400°F or 200°C.
2. Arrange tomato, eggplant, and zucchini slices in a baking dish in an alternate order.
3. Season with salt and pepper and drizzle with olive oil.
4. Bake until the vegetables are soft, about 20 minutes. Garnish it with fresh thyme.

Spanish Patatas Aioli

Instructions

- 4 medium-sized potatoes
- ¼ cup of mayonnaise
- 1 minced garlic clove
- 1 tablespoon of olive oil
- Salt and pepper as per your taste
- Fresh parsley

 Time: 25

 Servings: 3

 Calories: 160 Kcal

Instructions

1. Peel potatoes and cut them into cubes shape.
2. Then boil potatoes in salted water for 10-15 minutes until they are soft. After draining, let the potatoes cool down.
3. Combine them with olive oil, mayonnaise, and minced garlic in a bowl and stir until smooth to make aioli sauce.
4. Coat the potatoes thoroughly by tossing them with the aioli sauce.
5. Garnish it with parsley before serving.

Greek Baked Tomatoes

Ingredients

- 2 tablespoons of olive oil
- 4 large-sized tomatoes
- Salt and pepper as per your taste

Time: 20

Servings: 4

Calories: 50 Kcal

Instructions

1. Cut tomatoes into halves.
2. Then turn the oven on to 375°F, or 190°C. Arrange the tomatoes on a baking sheet, add salt and pepper to taste, and drizzle with olive oil.
3. Bake for 15 minutes until tomatoes get tender and juicy.

Turkish Grilled Eggplant Slices

Instructions

- 2 medium-sized eggplants
- 2 tablespoons of olive oil
- Salt and pepper as per your taste

Time: 15

Servings: 4

Calories: 80 Kcal

Instructions

1. Cut eggplant into normal-thickness slices.
2. Brush eggplant slices with olive oil and sprinkle with salt.
3. Grill or pan-fry over medium heat for 10 minutes, flipping halfway through.

French Roasted Artichokes

Ingredients

- 4 small-sized artichokes
- 2 tablespoons of olive oil
- Lemon wedges
- Salt and pepper as per your taste

Time: 25   Servings: 4   Calories: 90 Kcal

Instructions

1. Turn the oven on to 400°F or 200°C.
2. After putting the artichoke halves on a baking sheet, season them with salt and pepper and sprinkle them with olive oil.
3. Roast until soft and brown, about 20 minutes. Serve with wedges of lemon.

Greek Stewed Okra

Instructions

- ½ kg fresh okra
- 1 can (15oz) of chopped tomatoes
- Salt as per your taste

Time: 20   Servings: 4   Calories: 60 Kcal

Instructions

1. Trim okra into small pieces and chop tomatoes.
2. Put the tomatoes and okra in a pot. Simmer until the okra is soft, about 15 minutes.
3. Season it with salt and serve warm.

CHAPTER 11: WHOLE GRAINS, BEANS, AND PASTA

Mediterranean olive bread

Ingredients

 Time: 35

 Servings: 6

 KCAL Calories: 180 Kcal

- 2 cups of all-purpose flour
- 1 teaspoon of baking powder
- ½ teaspoon of salt
- ½ cup of chopped pitted olives
- ¼ cup olive oil and
- ¾ cup of hot water
- 1 tablespoon of fresh chopped rosemary

Instructions

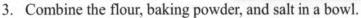

1. Turn the oven on to 400°F or 200°C.
2. Line a baking sheet with parchment paper or grease it.
3. Combine the flour, baking powder, and salt in a bowl.
4. Stir it while adding warm water and olive oil until a soft dough forms.
5. Add chopped rosemary and olives to the flour mixture and fold.
6. After the baking sheet is ready, form the dough into an oval or round loaf and put it on it.
7. Bake for 25 minutes or until the top is crusty and golden brown.

Mediterranean lentil loaf

Instructions

 Time: 60

 Servings: 6

 KCAL Calories: 180 Kcal

- 1 cup of cooked lentils
- ½ cup of chopped onion
- ¼ cup tomato paste
- 2 cups of breadcrumbs
- 1 tbl of olive oil
- 1 teaspoon of dried oregano

Instructions

1. Set the oven temperature to 175°C (350°F). Grease a pan.
2. Lentils, breadcrumbs, onion, tomato paste, olive oil, oregano, salt, and pepper should all be thoroughly mixed in a big basin.
3. Smooth the top of the loaf pan after pressing the mixture.
4. The loaf should be firm and have golden edges after 40 minutes of baking. Slice and serve.
5. Before slicing, allow it to cool slightly.

Turkish Bulgur with Tomato

Ingredients

- 1 cup of bulgur
- 1 can (15oz) of chopped tomatoes
- Salt as per your taste
- Coriander for garnishing

Time: 15

Servings: 4

Calories: 180 Kcal

Instructions

1. Put the bulgur and tomatoes in a saucepan.
2. Cook until the bulgur is soft, about 10 minutes on low heat.
3. Add salt for taste and garnish it with coriander.

Moroccan couscous with chickpeas

Instructions

- 1 cup of couscous
- 1 can of drained chickpeas
- 1 cup of vegetable broth
- Salt and pepper as per your taste

Time: 15

Servings: 4

Calories: 230 Kcal

Instructions

1. Boil the vegetable broth. Add the couscous to it and cover it for five minutes.
2. Add chickpeas, fluff the couscous, and season with salt and pepper.

Greek brown rice with dill

Ingredients

Time: 25

Servings: 4

KCAL
Calories: 150 Kcal

- 1 cup of brown rice
- 2 cups of vegetable broth
- 1 lemon juice
- 1 tablespoon of freshly chopped dill
- Salt as per your taste

Instructions

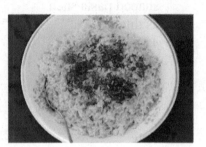

1. Cook rice in the vegetable broth. Add a tiny bit of salt.
2. Drizzle lemon juice on it before dishing, and garnish it with dill.

Lebanese Mujadara

Instructions

Time: 30

Servings: 4

KCAL
Calories: 220 Kcal

- 1 cup of brown lentils
- ½ cup of rice
- 4 cups of water
- Salt as per your taste

Instructions

1. Put all lentils in a pot and simmer it for 15 mins.
2. Then add rice and cook for 10 more minutes until the rice is done.
3. Serve them hot.

Italian Pasta e Fagioli

Ingredients

Time: 20   Servings: 4   Calories: 220 Kcal

- 1 cup of small-shaped pasta such as ditalini
- 4 cups of vegetable broth
- 1 can of drained cannellini beans
- Salt as per your taste

Instructions

1. In a pot, combine pasta, beans, and broth. Simmer for 10 to 15 minutes or until pasta is cooked.
2. Add salt and pepper for seasoning.

Lemon Garlic Shrimp Pasta

Instructions

Time: 25   Servings: 4   Calories: 180 Kcal

- 8 oz spaghetti
- ½ kg peeled shrimp
- 4 garlic cloves
- 3 tablespoons of olive oil
- 1 lemon juice and zest
- 1/4th cup parmesan cheese
- 1 teaspoon of red pepper flakes

Instructions

1. Cook spaghetti according to the packet's instructions. Drain it.
2. Add the garlic to heated oil and sauté for one minute.
3. Add shrimps and put spices. Cook for 2 to 3 minutes on each side.

4. Stir in spaghetti after adding lemon juice and zest.
5. Sprinkle parmesan cheese over the top. Serve warm.

CHAPTER 12: FISH AND SEAFOOD

Greek Grilled Sea Bass

Ingredients

 Time: 15   Servings: 2   Calories: 250 Kcal

- 2 fillets of sea bass
- 2 tablespoons of olive oil
- Juice of 1 lemon
- Salt and pepper as per your taste
- Oregano for garnishing

Instructions

1. Turn the grill on to medium-high heat.
2. Season Sea bass with salt, pepper, lemon juice, and olive oil.
3. Grill until cooked through, 4–5 minutes per side.
4. Garnish it with fresh oregano before dishing it out.

Italian lemon shrimp

Instructions

 Time: 10   Servings: 4   Calories: 150 Kcal

- 1/2kg shrimp
- 2 tablespoons of olive oil
- Juice of 1 lemon
- Salt and pepper as per your taste
- 2 garlic cloves (minced)
- Parsley

Instructions

1. Peel and devein the shrimp.
2. In a skillet, heat the olive oil over medium-high heat.
3. Cook the shrimp and garlic for two minutes on each side.
4. Add salt and pepper to the shrimp after you squeeze the lemon juice over them.
5. Garnish it with parsley.

Spanish garlic octopus

Ingredients

Time: 15

Servings: 4

KCAL
Calories: 180 Kcal

- 3 tablespoons of olive oil
- ½ kg of cooked octopus
- 3 thinly sliced garlic cloves
- Salt as per taste.
- Smoky paprika to taste

Instructions

1. Heat the olive oil in a skillet, add the garlic, and sauté until golden.
2. Sauté the octopus for three to four minutes.

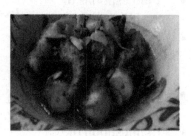

Moroccan Spiced Sardines

Instructions

Time: 13

Servings: 2

KCAL
Calories: 200 Kcal

- 6 fresh sardines
- 1 tablespoon of olive oil
- 1 teaspoon of cumin
- Salt and pepper as per your taste
- Fresh lemon wedges

Instructions

1. Marinate sardines with salt, pepper, cumin, and olive oil.
2. Then pan-fry or grill them for 3–4 minutes on each side.
3. Serve them with wedges of fresh lemon.

Greek Lemon Herb Salmon

Ingredients

Time: 20

Servings: 4

KCAL

Calories: 250 Kcal

- 4 salmon fillets
- 2 tablespoons of fresh lime juice
- 1 tablespoon of chopped rosemary
- 2 tablespoons of olive oil
- 1 tablespoon of chopped thyme
- Salt and pepper as per your taste
- Lemon slices

Instructions

1. Set the oven's temperature to 400°F or 200°C.
2. Arrange the salmon fillets on a piece of butter paper and place them on the baking pan.
3. In a small bowl, combine the lemon juice, olive oil, thyme, rosemary, salt, and pepper.
4. Drizzle the salmon fillets with the mixture.

Italian Anchovy Spaghetti

Instructions

Time: 15

Servings: 2

KCAL

Calories: 350 Kcal

- 4 oz spaghetti
- 1 tablespoon of olive oil
- 4 fillets of anchovy
- 1 minced garlic clove
- Fresh parsley

Instructions

1. Cook spaghetti (follow the instructions mentioned on the spaghetti packet)
2. Drain water from spaghetti.
3. Chop fillets of anchovy into small pieces.
4. Add the garlic and anchovies to heated olive oil and simmer until aromatic.
5. Add parsley as a garnish and toss spaghetti with anchovy sauce.

Shrimp Soup

Ingredients

- ½ kg peeled shrimp
- 3 minced garlic cloves
- Salt and pepper as per your taste
- ½ cup white wine
- 3 cups of vegetable broth

Time: 25

Servings: 4

Calories: 110 Kcal

Instructions

1. Put wine, vegetable broth, and garlic in a pot. Let all the ingredients to simmer.
2. Add shrimp and simmer for 3–4 minutes or until pink.
3. Add salt and pepper for seasoning.

Mediterranean Turkey skillet

Instructions

- ½ kg minced Turkey
- 1 red bell pepper
- 1 zucchini
- ½ cup tomatoes
- 1/4th cup of feta cheese
- 1 tablespoon of olive oil
- Fresh parsley
- Salt, oregano, and pepper as per your taste

Time: 20

Servings: 4

Calories: 240 Kcal

Instructions

1. Dice bell pepper, zucchini, and tomatoes. Set them aside.
2. Then, in a skillet, heat the olive oil over medium heat. Add the ground turkey and cook for 5 to 7 minutes.
3. Stir and turn it often until the minced turkey gets brown.
4. Add the cherry tomatoes, red bell pepper, zucchini, oregano, and salt and pepper.
5. Sauté until the vegetables are soft.
6. Sprinkle it with fresh parsley and feta cheese.

Lemon Chicken

Ingredients

Time: 40

Servings: 4

Calories: 250 Kcal

- 2 tablespoons of olive oil
- 4 chicken thighs
- Juice of 1 lemon
- 1 tsp oregano
- Salt and pepper as per your taste
- Salad leaves
- Lemon slices

Instructions

1. Turn the oven on to 400°F or 200°C.
2. Combine the oregano, lemon juice, olive oil, salt, and pepper in a bowl.
3. Apply the mixture to the chicken.
4. The chicken should be baked for 25 to 30 minutes till it gets tender.
5. Serve it with lemon slices and salad leaves.

Spicy Harissa Chicken Skewers

Instructions

Time: 25

Servings: 4

Calories: 220 Kcal

- 1/2 kg chicken breast
- 1 tablespoon of olive oil
- 2 tablespoons of harissa paste
- Salt and pepper as per your taste
- Skewers
- Onion, tomato and cucumber slices

Instructions

1. Cut the chicken breast into small cubes.
2. Combine the chicken, salt, olive oil, and harissa paste in a bowl.
3. Thread the chicken and vegetable slices on the skewers alternatively.
4. Cook on a grill or broiler for 10 to 15 minutes.

Italian Meatballs

Ingredients

- ½ cup of breadcrumbs
- ½ kg grounded Beef1/4th cup of parmesan cheese
- 1 egg
- 1 tablespoon of olive oil
- Salt and pepper as per your taste

Time: 30

Servings: 4

Calories: 300 Kcal

Instructions

1. Preheat oven to 400°F (200°C).
2. In a bowl, put all the ingredients. Mix and then knead the ground beef.
3. Mold the mixture into even circular-shaped balls.
4. Place them on a baking sheet.
5. Bake for 20 minutes and serve them warm.

Moroccan Chicken Tagine

Instructions

- ½ kg chicken thighs
- 1 can chickpeas
- 1 onion
- 1 teaspoon of cumin
- 1 teaspoon of cinnamon
- Salt and pepper as per your taste

Time: 50

Servings: 4

Calories: 320 Kcal

Instructions

1. Add the onion and cook until it becomes tender.
2. Add the chickpeas, chicken, and seasonings. Cook for five minutes.
3. After adding 2 cups of water, simmer for 30 minutes with a lid on.

Cypriot Chicken with Herbs

Ingredients

- 2 tablespoons of olive oil
- 4 chicken drumsticks
- Juice of 1 lemon
- 1 teaspoon thyme
- Salt and pepper as per your tase

Time: 35

Servings: 4

Calories: 270 Kcal

Instructions

1. Turn the oven on to 400°F or 200°C.
2. Combine salt, pepper, lemon juice, thyme, and olive oil.
3. Coat the chicken with the mixture.
4. Bake for 25 mins until well done.

Italian Chicken Piccata

Instructions

- 4 chicken breasts
- ¼ cup of flour
- ¼ cup of lemon juice
- ¼ cup of capers
- 3 tablespoons of olive oil
- Salt and pepper as per your taste

Time: 30

Servings: 4

Calories: 320 Kcal

Instructions

1. Season chicken with salt and pepper.
2. Then, toss it thoroughly in the after flour.
3. Cook the chicken in a skillet with hot oil for 5 to 7 minutes on each side or until brown.
4. Simmer for three minutes after adding the lemon juice and capers.

Lebanese Shish Tawook

Ingredients

- ½ kg chicken breast, cubed
- 2 tablespoons of yoghurt
- 1 tablespoon of lemon juice
- 1 tablespoon of garlic powder
- Salt and pepper as per your taste
- Red and yellow bell pepper cubes
- Skewers

 Time: 25

 Servings: 4

 Calories: 230 Kcal

Instructions

1. Combine yoghurt, lemon juice, salt, pepper, and garlic powder in a bowl.
2. For ten minutes, add the chicken and marinate it.
3. After threading chicken and bell peppers onto skewers, cook for 10-15 mins.

Spanish Chorizo Hash

Instructions

- 8 oz of Spanish chorizo
- 2 potatoes
- 1 onion
- 1 red bell pepper
- 2 tablespoons of olive oil
- 2 cloves of minced garlic
- Salt and pepper as per your taste
- Fresh parsley

 Time: 30

 Servings: 4

 Calories: 320 Kcal

Instructions

1. Dice potatoes, chop onion and bell pepper, and mince garlic.
2. Heat olive oil and sauté potatoes in a skillet for 10 to 12 minutes. Then, put them aside.
3. Add the chorizo to the same skillet and cook for 5 minutes.
4. Sauté the garlic, bell pepper, and onion for 3-5 mins.
5. Put the potatoes back in the skillet, stir, and heat for 2-3 mins.

Turkish Adana Kebab

Ingredients

 Time: 30

 Servings: 4

 Calories: 290 Kcal

- ½ kg ground lamb
- 1 onion
- Coriander
- 1 teaspoon red pepper flakes
- Salt and pepper as per your taste
- Skewers

Instructions

1. Put the ground lamb in a bowl. Add spices, coriander, and grated onion.
2. Mix them well. Shape them into long kebabs on skewers.
3. You can grease your palm with oil or water.
4. Grill for 10-15 minutes until cooked.

CHAPTER 14: EGG DISHES

Shakshuka

Time: 25   Servings: 4   Calories: 160 Kcal

Ingredients

- 1 tablespoon of olive oil
- 4 eggs
- 1½ teaspoon of chilli powder
- 2 large chopped tomatoes
- 1 teaspoon of ground cumin
- 1 tsp of paprika
- 1 chopped onion
- 1 sliced red bell pepper
- 2 garlic cloves
- Salt and pepper

Instructions

1. Take a frying pan. Add olive oil and sauté onion, bell pepper, and garlic. Cook until these ingredients become soft.
2. Add on the spices.
3. Put finely chopped tomatoes in it and simmer it for 5-7mins.
4. When the sauce is ready, crack eggs on it and let it cook in steam for 2-3 min.
5. Garnish it with parsley and serve.

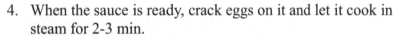

Egg muffins

Time: 30   Servings: 6   Calories: 70 Kcal

Instructions

- 6 eggs
- 1/4 cup of spinach, chopped
- 1/4 cup of bell peppers, chopped
- 1/4 cup chopped cherry tomatoes
- 1/4 cup of crumbled feta cheese

Instructions

1. Grease a muffin tray and preheat the oven to 350°F (175°C).
2. Add the spinach, bell pepper, tomatoes, and feta to a bowl with whisked eggs.
3. Fill muffin tins, then bake for 18 to 20 minutes.

Eggs and Greek Yoghurt Salad

Ingredients

Time: 10

Servings: 2

Calories: 200 Kcal

- 4 boiled eggs.
- 1 teaspoon of olive oil
- Salt and pepper as per your taste
- 1/4th cup of Greek yogurt

Instructions

1. Chop boiled eggs and put them in a bowl.
2. Season it with olive oil, salt and pepper.
3. Add Greek yoghurt and mix it with the eggs gently. Then serve.

Eggs with Za'atar

Instructions

Time: 10

Servings: 2

Calories: 180 Kcal

- 4 eggs
- 1 tablespoon of olive oil
- 1 teaspoon of Za'atar spice
- Salt as per your taste

Instructions

1. Put a skillet on the stove.
2. Warm olive oil and then half fry the eggs.
3. Sprinkle salt and za'atar spice over it.

Italian Frittata

Ingredients

- 4 eggs
- ½ cup spinach
- ¼ cup cheese
- Olive oil
- Salt and pepper as per your taste

Time: 15

Servings: 4

Calories: 130 Kcal

Instructions

1. Chop spinach and crumble the cheese.
2. Whisk eggs in a bowl. Then, add spinach, cheese, and seasonings.
3. Brush olive oil on a nonstick pan and pour the mixture into it.
4. Cook on low flame until it is set.

Turkish Cilbir

Instructions

- 4 eggs
- Vinegar
- 1/4th cup of Greek yoghurt
- Salt and pepper as per your taste

Time: 10

Servings: 2

Calories: 160 Kcal

Instructions

1. Heat water in a pot until it gently simmers to make poached eggs.
2. Add a dash of vinegar to it.
3. Crack an egg into a cup, slide it into the water, and cook for 3-4 minutes until whites are set.
4. Place poached eggs on yoghurt, and it is ready to be served.

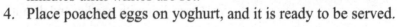

Italian Eggs in Purgatory

Ingredients

Time: 15

Servings: 2

KCAL

Calories: 130 Kcal

- 4 eggs
- 4 medium-sized tomatoes
- 1 minced garlic clove
- Salt and pepper as per your taste
- Parsley.

Instructions

1. Brush the skillet with olive oil. Put garlic and tomatoes in it.
2. Let the mixture simmer for 5-6 minutes until the texture smooths. It will make purgatory.
3. Crack eggs on top of purgatory and heat until the whites are set.

Moroccan Spiced Poached Eggs

Instructions

Time: 15

Servings: 2

KCAL

Calories: 140 Kcal

- 4 eggs
- 1 can of diced tomatoes
- 1 teaspoon of cumin
- Salt and pepper as per your taste
- Parsley.

Instructions

1. Heat water in a pot until it gently simmers to make poached eggs.
2. Add a dash of vinegar to it.
3. Crack an egg into a cup, slide it into the water, and cook for 3-4 minutes until whites are set.
4. Now heat diced tomatoes in a pan and add cumin seeds in it. Let them simmer. Put poached eggs over it and add seasonings.
5. Garnish it with parsley and dish it out.

Chicken and Egg Sandwich

Ingredients

Time: 25

Servings: 1

Calories: 160 Kcal

- 1 egg
- 2 slices of whole wheat bread
- 50g cooked chicken breast, shredded
- 1 tablespoon light mayonnaise
- Salt and pepper as per your taste
- Lettuce leaves

Instructions

1. Boil the egg and crumble it.
2. Make shreds of boiled chicken.
3. Then, put both ingredients in a bowl and mix it with mayonnaise and seasonings.
4. Layer lettuce, chicken mixture, and egg on toasted bread.
5. Top with another slice, cut in half, and serve.

Egg and Veggies Omelet

Instructions

Time: 10

Servings: 1

Calories: 145 Kcal

- 2 eggs
- 1 teaspoon of olive oil
- ¼ cup of chopped veggies (bell pepper, onion, tomato)
- Salt and pepper as per your taste

Instructions

1. Finely chop vegetables. Then, put a frying pan on the stove.
2. Add olive oil and sauté vegetables.
3. Then, crack eggs in the pan and whisk it with vegetables.
4. Add salt and pepper to taste.
5. Serve the omelette.

Italian Focaccia

Ingredients

- 2 cups of flour
- 1 cup warm water
- 2 tablespoons of olive oil
- Rosemary

Time: 30

Servings: 6

Calories: 180 Kcal

Instructions

1. Make a dough by combining flour, water, and 1 tablespoon of olive oil.
2. Spread in a baking dish, top with the remaining olive oil, season with salt and rosemary, and bake for 20 minutes at 400°F (200°C).

Lebanese Manakaish

Instructions

- 2 cups of flour
- 1 cup warm water
- 1 tablespoon of olive oil
- 2 tablespoons of za'atar seasoning

Time: 20

Servings: 4

Calories: 190 Kcal

Instructions

1. Mix up all the ingredients and make a fine dough mixture. Roll the dough into a flatbread shape.
2. Drizzle it with olive oil and sprinkle za'atar on it.
3. Bake for 10 minutes at 375°F (190°C). Then serve oven-fresh.

Pita bread

Ingredients

- 2 cups of flour
- 1 cup warm water
- 1 teaspoon of salt
- 1 tablespoon of olive oil

 Time: 20

 Servings: 6

 Calories: 150 Kcal

Instructions

1. Combine all the ingredients. Knead it well until there are no lumps in the dough.
2. Now, shape the dough into balls.
3. Roll the ball into flatbread. Use a rolling pin and board.
4. You can also roll it over the kitchen counter.
5. Cook each side of the flatbread on a heated skillet until it puffs up.

Spanish coca flatbread

Instructions

- 2 cups of flour
- 1 cup warm water
- 1 teaspoon of salt
- 1 tablespoon of olive oil
- Thyme and olives

 Time: 40

 Servings: 4

 Calories: 190 Kcal

Instructions

1. Combine all the ingredients. Knead it well until there are no lumps in the dough.
2. Spread it on a baking sheet.
3. Brush olive oil over it and sprinkle thyme and olives.
4. Put it in the oven and bake at 400°F (200°C) for 25 minutes.

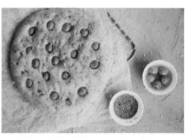

Italian Pizza

Ingredients

- 1½ all-purpose flour
- ½ cup warm water
- ½ tsp of salt
- 1 tbl of olive oil
- 1 tsp of yeast
- ½ cup of tomato sauce
- ½ cup of mozzarella cheese
- Oregano
- ½ cup of cheddar cheese
- Fresh basil leaves

Time: 35

Servings: 4

KCAL

Calories: 250 Kcal

Instructions

1. Combine the sugar, yeast, and water in a large bowl. Give it 5 mins to sit.
2. Then, add flour, salt, and olive oil to it.
3. Knead the dough for 5-10 mins. Cover the dough and place it in a warm place for an hour until it doubles.
4. When it is risen, make it through a rolling pin.
5. Spread tomato sauce over the rolled-out dough, then sprinkle cheese and basil leaves.
6. Bake in a preheated oven for 10 to 15 minutes at 475°F.

Khobz bread

Instructions

- 2 cups of flour
- 1 cup warm water
- 1 teaspoon of sugar
- 1 teaspoon of salt
- 1 tablespoon of olive oil
- 1 teaspoon of yeast

Time: 35

Servings: 6

KCAL

Calories: 120 Kcal

Instructions

1. Combine the sugar, yeast, and water in a large bowl. Give it 5 mins to sit.
2. Then, add flour, salt, and olive oil to it.
3. Knead the dough for 5-10 mins.
4. Make balls of dough. Flatten it with your hands. Place it in a warm place for an hour until it doubles.
5. Preheat the oven to 400°F (200°C) before baking. Place the flattened balls on the baking sheet. Then bake for 20 minutes or until golden brown.

French tarte flambee

Ingredients

- 1 thin pizza crust
- ½ cup of sour cream
- ½ cup of thinly sliced onions
- ½ cup of chopped bacon
- Salt and pepper as per your taste
- Fresh chives

Time: 20

Servings: 4

Calories: 270 Kcal

Instructions

1. Set the oven temperature to 475°F (245°C). Cover the crust with sour cream, then add the bacon and onions. Add a little salt and pepper for seasoning.
2. Put the tarte inside the oven.
3. Bake it for ten minutes till the edges are golden and crispy.
4. Garnish with chives and cut into serving slices.

Lebanese shawarma wrap

Instructions

- 4 pita bread
- 1/2kg chicken breast (thinly cut)
- 1 tablespoon of olive oil
- 1 teaspoon of ground cumin
- 1 teaspoon of paprika
- ½ cup of shredded lettuce
- Salt and pepper as per your taste

Time:15

Servings: 4

Calories: 350 Kcal

Instructions

1. Cook the chicken by heating the olive oil in a skillet over medium heat.
2. Add chicken slices and seasoning (salt, pepper, paprika, and cumin).
3. Put the pita bread on a plate. Spread sauce over it and top it with the cooked chicken, lettuce, and tomatoes.
4. Then, wrap the pita bread and serve warm.

Italian calzone

Ingredients

Time: 35

Servings: 4

Calories: 350 Kcal

- Pizza dough
- 1 cup mozzarella cheese
- Oregano
- ½ cup tomato sauce
- Salt and pepper as per your taste

Instructions

1. Roll the dough into a flat shape.
2. Then, cut into two halves.
3. Fill half the bread with cheese, tomato sauce, and seasonings.
4. Fold it and turn it into a triangular shape.
5. Bake these calzones at 400°F (200°C) for 20 mins.

Cypriot Halloumi Pita

Instructions

Time: 20

Servings: 4

Calories: 200 Kcal

- 4 pita breads
- 1 cup of diced halloumi cheese
- Oregano
- Tomato slices
- 1 teaspoon of olive oil
- Salt and pepper as per your taste

Instructions

1. Warm pita bread in a pan.
2. Put tomato slices and halloumi cheese on half pita bread.
3. Drizzle olive oil on it and sprinkle the spices.
4. Fold the pita bread and enjoy.

CHAPTER 16: DESSERTS

Spanish flan

Ingredients

- 1 cup of sugar
- 4 large-sized eggs
- 1 can condensed milk
- 1 cup evaporated milk

Time: 50

Servings: 4

Calories: 300 Kcal

Instructions

1. Put sugar in a pan. Melt it until it gets caramelized. Pour the caramel into a mold.
2. Blend condensed milk, evaporated milk, and eggs in a separate bowl.
3. Now, pour this mixture above the caramel sauce into the mold.
4. Put it in the oven and let it bake at 350°F for 40 minutes.
5. Put a plate over the mold and take out the flan in an upside-down way.
6. The caramel layer will be on top after dishing out.

French Canelés

Instructions

- 1 egg
- 1 cup of milk
- ½ cup of all-purpose flour
- ½ cup powdered sugar
- Chocolate sprinkle

Time: 60

Servings: 4

Calories: 220 Kcal

Instructions

1. Blend egg first in a bowl. Then, add flour, powdered sugar, and milk. The addition of milk can adjust the consistency of the batter.
2. Pour the mixture into the mold and bake at 400°F for 50 minutes.
3. Dish it out and garnish it with chocolate sprinkles..

Lebanese Rice Pudding

Ingredients

Time: 25

Servings: 4

Calories: 260 Kcal

- 1 cup of short-grain rice
- 1-2 teaspoons of rose water
- 2 tablespoons of cornstarch (dissolved in 1/4 cup cold milk)
- 1 teaspoon of vanilla extract
- 4 cups of milk
- 1/4th cup of sugar
- Pistachio granulated

Instructions

1. In a pot, combine the rice and milk. Cook over medium heat.
2. Stir the mixture constantly after 2-3 minutes until the rice is tender.
3. Add sugar and stir to dissolve it.
4. Then, add the cornstarch mixture and continue stirring.
5. Wait for 5 minutes or until the pudding thickens.
6. After adding the vanilla extract or rose water, cook for a further one to two minutes.
7. Dish out it in a bowl and garnish it with pistachio. Serve.

Spanish Torrijas

Instructions

Time: 15

Servings: 4

Calories: 220 Kcal

- 4 bread slices.
- 1 cup milk
- 1 beaten egg
- 1 tablespoon of cinnamon sugar (mixture of cinnamon powder and granulated sugar)
- Olive oil

Instructions

1. Infuse the bread slice in milk.
2. Then thoroughly, dip them in the beaten eggs.
3. Fry the bread slices in a pan with olive oil.
4. Let it cook until the slice gets golden on each side.
5. Sprinkle cinnamon sugar on it and serve.

Greek Semolina Halwa

Ingredients

Time: 40

Servings: 8

Calories: 220 Kcal

- 1 cup of semolina
- 1 cup sugar
- 1 cups of water
- ½ cup vegetable oil
- 1 teaspoon of vanilla extract
- ¼ cup chopped almonds and walnuts

Instructions

1. In a saucepan, combine the sugar and water.
2. Let the mixture get boiled. Then, put it aside.
3. Take a skillet, warm the vegetable oil and sauté the semolina until its colour turns golden. After cooking the semolina in oil, gradually pour the sugar syrup into it.
4. Add nuts and vanilla extract.
5. Cook it until the consistency gets thick.
6. Dish it out onto a greased plate.
7. After 2 hours, cut it into squares and serve.

CHAPTER 7: MEAL PLAN AND GROCERY LIST

CHAPTER 17: 30-DAY MEAL PLAN AND GROCERY LIST

Week 1

Days	Breakfast	Lunch	Dinner	Snack
Day 1	Shakshuka	Hummus and vegetable wrap	Turkish red lentil soup	Marinated olives
Day 2	Avocado toast with feta and tomato	Spanish Gazpacho	Italian Anchovy Pasta	Caprese skewers
Day 3	Egg sandwiches with rosemary, feta and tomato	Greek Lemon Herb Salmon	French tarte flambee	Stuffed grapes leaves (Dolmas)
Day 4	Grilled halloumi and tomato stack	Mediterranean lentil loaf	Italian pizza	Greek spinach pie (Sapanakopita)
Day 5	Berry-almond smoothie bowl	Greek Grilled Sea Bass	Italian Minestrone	Falafel balls
Day 6	Mediterranean Frittata	Italian lemon and garlic shrimp	Moroccan couscous with chickpeas	Mediterranean tomato brochette
Day 7	Hummus and vegetable wrap	Spanish Gazpacho	Spanish garlic octopus	Greek cucumber cups

Week 2

Days	Breakfast	Lunch	Dinner	Snack
Day 1	Egg and Veggies Omelet	Lebanese shawarma wrap	Turkish Adana Kebab	Turkish grilled eggplant slices
Day 2	Moroccan Spiced Poached Eggs	Spanish Chorizo and Potato Hash	Italian calzone	French roasted artichokes
Day 3	Italian Frittata	Cypriot Halloumi Pita	Italian Chicken Piccata	5Moroccan carrot salad
Day 4	Eggs with Za'atar	Lebanese Shish Tawook	Spicy Harissa Chicken Skewers	Mediterranean chickpea salad
Day 5	Spanish Tortilla de Patatas	Mediterranean Turkey skillet	French Bouillabaisse-Inspired Shrimp Soup	Greek baked tomatoes
Day 6	Shakshuka	Moroccan Chicken Tagine	Italian Meatballs	Lebanese roasted cauliflower
Day 7	Egg muffins	Cypriot Chicken with Lemon and Herbs	Mediterranean Lemon Chicken	Italian sauteed zucchini

Week 3

Days	Breakfast	Lunch	Dinner	Snack
Day 1	Berry-almond smoothie bowl	Tomato basil soup	Greek Grilled Sea Bass	Greek cucumber cups
Day 2	Mediterranean Frittata	Greek lemon chickpea soup	Lebanese lentil soup	Falafel balls
Day 3	Hummus and vegetable wrap	Italian Pasta e Fagioli	Italian lemon and garlic shrimp	Greek spinach pie (Sapanakopita)
Day 4	Spinach and feta omelette	Italian Ribollita	Italian Chicken Piccata	Mediterranean tomato brochette
Day 5	Quinoa bowl	Mediterranean Turkey skillet	Italian Anchovy Pasta	Tabbouleh
Day 6	Egg muffins	Lebanese Shish Tawook	Moroccan couscous with chickpeas	Cucumber yogurt salad
Day 7	Italian Frittata	French Coq au Vin	Spanish Chorizo and Potato Hash	Caprese salad

Week 4

Days	Breakfast	Lunch	Dinner	Snack
Day 1	Shakshuka	Lebanese lentil soup	Mediterranean lentil loaf	Caprese skewers
Day 2	Grilled halloumi and tomato stack	Italian Chicken Piccata	Italian Meatballs	Stuffed grapes leaves (Dolmas)
Day 3	Spinach and feta omelette	Mediterranean Turkey skillet	Italian Pasta e Fagioli	Falafel balls
Day 4	Avocado toast with feta and tomato	French Coq au Vin	French Bouillabaisse-Inspired Shrimp Soup	Cucumber yogurt salad
Day 5	Quinoa bowl	Cypriot Chicken with Lemon and Herbs	Spanish Gazpacho	Spanish grilled bell peppers
Day 6	Egg muffins	Spanish Chorizo and Potato Hash	Lebanese Shish Tawook	Mediterranean chickpea salad
Day 7	Egg sandwiches with rosemary, feta and tomato	Turkish red lentil soup	Greek Grilled Sea Bass	Greek spinach pie (Sapanakopita)
Bonus Days				
1	Mediterranean Frittata	Lebanese Shish Tawook	Italian Chicken Piccata	Caprese skewers
2	Egg muffins	Cypriot Chicken with Lemon and Herbs	Moroccan couscous with chickpeas	Tabbouleh

GROCERY LIST

WEEK 1

Grains

4 oz pasta

1 cup of couscous

1/2 cup of elbow macaroni or pasta shells

2 tortilla made of whole grains

1 thin pizza crust

3 cups all-purpose flour

1 cup red lentils

Fruits

Fresh lemon wedges

10 ripe tomatoes

35 cherry tomatoes

1 avocado

1 cup mixed berries

1 banana

Vegetables

7 onion

1 1/2 zucchini

3 carrots

2 celery stalks

3 large-sized cucumber

1 green bell pepper

15-17 garlic cloves

2 red bell pepper

2 1/2 cup of spinach

Dairy

1 ½ cup of crumbled feta cheese

½ cup of Greek yogurt

½ cup almond milk

10 eggs

3 slices of halloumi cheese

½ cup of mozzarella cheese

16 balls of fresh mozzarella

½ cup of cheddar cheese

½ cup of sour cream

Meats or Protein

6 fresh sardines

½ kg of cooked octopus

4 fillets of anchovy

1/2 cup of chopped bacon

Bread

2 cups of bread crumbs

6 baguette slices

3 whole-grain bread slice

Herbs and Seasonings

Olive oil

Cumin (multiple entries)

Salt and pepper (multiple entries)

Smoky paprika to taste

Dill

Dried oregano

Dried basil

Ground cumin

Balsamic glaze

1 tablespoon of lemon zest

Fresh rosemary

Chili powder

Fresh basil

Fresh chives

Canned Goods or Pre-Packaged Foods

1 can (15 oz) diced tomatoes

9 cup of vegetable broth

1 cup of tomato sauce

20 jarred grape leaves

1 cup of cooked lentils

1 can (15 oz) kidney beans

2 can of drained chickpeas

1 cup of cooked rice

Others

1/2 cup Hummus

Pine nuts

Currants

¼ cup granola

1 tablespoon of almonds

1 teaspoon of yeast

6 sheets of phyllo pastry

WEEK 2

Grains

8 pita bread

1 Pizza dough

½ cup breadcrumbs

¼ cup of flour

Fruits

Lemon wedges

Vegetables

½ cup of shredded lettuce

1/2 cucumber

1/4 cup capers

1 cup spinach

14 tomatoes

8- 9 onion

4 red bell pepper

2 potatoes

3 medium-sized eggplants

5 zucchinis

4 small-sized artichokes

1 cauliflower head

1 1/4 cup of cherry tomatoes

Dairy

1 cup mozzarella cheese

1 cup diced halloumi cheese

¼ cup of cheese (type not specified)

1/2 cup of crumbled feta cheese

¼ cup of parmesan cheese

1/4 cup of Greek yogurt

29 eggs

Yogurt

Meats or Protein

1 ½ kg chicken breast (cut)

8 chicken thigh

4 chicken drumsticks

1/2 kg chicken thighs

½ kg ground lamb

1/2 kg ground beef

8 oz of Spanish chorizo

½ kg minced turkey

½ kg peeled shrimp

Herbs and Seasonings

Olive oil (multiple entries)

Ground cumin (multiple entries)

Paprika (multiple entries)

Salt and pepper (multiple entries)

Oregano (multiple entries)

1 teaspoon of Za'atar spice

Coriander

Red pepper flakes

Chili powder

Cinnamon

Fresh parsley

Fresh thyme

Garlic powder

Canned Goods or Pre-Packaged Foods

1 can of diced tomatoes

1/2 cup tomato sauce

2 can chickpeas

3 cups of vegetable broth

½ cup white wine

Others

2 tablespoon of harissa paste

7 garlic cloves

Juice of lemon (multiple entries)

Skewers

WEEK 3

Grains

1 cup cooked bulgur

1 cup of couscous

1 cup of small-shaped pasta such as ditalini

2 cups of stale bread chunks

4 oz pasta

1/2 cup of flour

1 tortilla made of whole grains

1 cup red lentils

6 sheets of phyllo pastry

1/4 cup granola

6 baguette slices

Fruit

½ sliced banana

1 cup mixed berries

1/4 sliced avocado

Vegetables

5 onions

4 red bell pepper

1 1/2 zucchini

3 cucumber

3 large-sized tomatoes

3 cup of diced cherry tomatoes

3 1/2 cup of spinach chopped

2 potatoes

12 garlic cloves

Dairy

1½ cup of crumbled feta cheese

1 cup fresh mozzarella

¼ cup sliced feta cheese

1 ½ cup Greek yogurt

2 tablespoon yogurt

¼ cup of cheese (type not specified)

17 eggs

1/2 cup almond milk

Meats or Protein

½ kg minced turkey

6 chicken breasts

4 chicken thighs

2 fillets of sea bass

½ kg shrimp

8 oz of Spanish chorizo

Herbs and Seasonings

Olive oil (multiple entries)

Salt and pepper (multiple entries)

Cumin powder (multiple entries)

Ground cumin (multiple entries)

Fresh parsley (multiple entries)

Basil

Garlic powder

1 tablespoon of red wine vinegar

Freshly chopped dill (multiple entries)

Oregano for garnishing

Ground coriander

lemon juice (multiple entries)

Harissa paste

1 tablespoon of capers

Canned Goods or Pre-Packaged Foods

3 can of drained chickpeas

16 cups of vegetable broth

1 cup chicken broth

1 can (15oz) drained cannellini beans

1 can (15oz) white beans

1 can (15oz) chopped tomatoes

1 can (28 ounces) crushed tomatoes

Others

3 tablespoons of hummus

2 tablespoon of chopped olives

Skewers

1 tablespoon almonds

WEEK 4

Grains

2 ½ cup of breadcrumbs

1/2 cup of flour

1 cup of small-shaped pasta such as ditalini

1 cup of cooked lentils

1 cup of cooked rice

½ cup of cooked quinoa

2 cups of bread crumbs

6 sheets of phyllo pastry

Fruits

1 lemon

3 ½ cup of cherry tomatoes

1/2 avocado

Vegetables

2 potatoes

1 green bell pepper

13 tomatoes

11 onion

3 red bell pepper

1 zucchini

3 cucumber

1 carrot

3 cup spinach

15 garlic cloves

Dairy

1/4th cup of parmesan cheese

1 cup Greek yogurt

¼ cup crumbled feta cheese

2 tablespoons of shredded feta cheese

1/4 cup sliced feta cheese

3 slices of halloumi cheese

16 balls of fresh mozzarella

Meats or Protein

½ kg grounded beef

8 oz of Spanish chorizo

4 chicken thigh

6 chicken breasts

4 chicken drumsticks

½ kg peeled shrimp

2 fillets of sea bass

20 jarred grape leaves

15 eggs

Bread

3 whole-grain bread slice

Herbs and Seasonings

Salt and pepper as per your taste

Olive oil (listed multiple times)

Fresh parsley

Fresh dill

Thyme

Ground cumin

Ground coriander

Paprika

Chili powder

Balsamic glaze

Red wine vinegar

Garlic powder

Fresh basil

Canned Goods or Pre-Packaged Foods

1 can of drained cannellini beans

2 can of drained chickpeas

17 cups of vegetable broth

1 cup chicken broth

1/2 cup tomato paste

Others

Skewers

Pine nuts

Currants

Lemon juice

½ cup white wine

BONUS DAYS

Grains

1/4 cup flour

1 cup of couscous

1 cup of cooked bulgur

Vegetables

1 1/4 cup red amd yellow bell pepper

2.5 cups cherry tomatoes

1/2 onions

1/2 zucchini

1 cup Fresh parsley

1/4 cup spinach

1 cup of vegetable broth

Dairy

1/2 cup fetta cheese

2 Tablespoon yogurt

16 balls of fresh mozzarella

Meats or ptotein

10 large eggs

1.2 kg chicken breast

4 chicken drumsticks

Bread

Herbs and seasoning

Olive oil

Salt and pepper

1 tablespoon garlic powder

16 fresh basil leaves

1 teaspoon thyme

Canned Goods or Pre-Packaged Foods

1 can of drained chickpeas

Others

Lemon juice

Skewers

1/4 cup capers

1 tablespoon balsamic glaze

REFERENCES

1. Hidalgo-Mora JJ, García-Vigara A, Sánchez-Sánchez ML, García-Pérez MÁ, Tarín J, Cano A. The Mediterranean diet: A historical perspective on food for health. Maturitas. 2020 Feb 1;132:65–9.

2. Endorphins: What They Are and Why They're Important [Internet]. [cited 2024 Oct 26]. Available from: https://www.verywellhealth.com/endorphins-definition-5189854

3. Capurso A. The Mediterranean diet: a historical perspective. Aging Clin Exp Res [Internet]. 2024 Dec 1 [cited 2024 Oct 21];36(1):1–6. Available from: https://link.springer.com/article/10.1007/s40520-023-02686-3

4. Ancel Keys - Seven Countries Study | The first study to relate diet with cardiovascular disease. [Internet]. [cited 2024 Oct 21]. Available from: https://www.sevencountriesstudy.com/about-the-study/investigators/ancel-keys/

5. Wei Z, Li W, Lei C, Caixia A, Chuan Z, Jianqin W. Maternal seafood consumption and fetal growth: a birth cohort study in urban China. BMC Pregnancy Childbirth [Internet]. 2023 Dec 1 [cited 2023 Oct 25];23(1):1–11. Available from: https://bmcpregnancychildbirth.biomedcentral.com/articles/10.1186/s12884-023-05431-w

6. Mediterranean Diet: Food List & Meal Plan. Available from: https://my.clevelandclinic.org/health/articles/16037-mediterranean-diet

7. Omar SH. Cardioprotective and neuroprotective roles of oleuropein in olive. Saudi Pharm J. 2010 Jul 1;18(3):111–21.

8. Innes JK, Calder PC. Marine Omega-3 (N-3) Fatty Acids for Cardiovascular Health: An Update for 2020. Int J Mol Sci [Internet]. 2020 Feb 2 [cited 2023 Oct 25];21(4). Available from: https://pubmed.ncbi.nlm.nih.gov/32085487/

9. Tong TYN, Appleby PN, Bradbury KE, Perez-Cornago A, Travis RC, Clarke R, et al. Risks of ischaemic heart disease and stroke in meat eaters, fish eaters, and vegetarians over 18 years of follow-up: results from the prospective EPIC-Oxford study. BMJ [Internet]. 2019 [cited 2023 Oct 25];366. Available from: https://pubmed.ncbi.nlm.nih.gov/31484644/

10. Cremonini AL, Caffa I, Cea M, Nencioni A, Odetti P, Monacelli F. Nutrients in the Prevention of Alzheimer's Disease. Oxid Med Cell Longev [Internet]. 2019 [cited 2024 Oct 22];2019:9874159. Available from: https://pmc.ncbi.nlm.nih.gov/articles/PMC6746160/

11. MIND Diet – The Nutrition Source [Internet]. [cited 2024 Oct 22]. Available from: https://nutritionsource.hsph.harvard.edu/healthy-weight/diet-reviews/mind-diet/

12. Sidossis LS, Lawson R, Aprilakis E, Barata BC, Baska A, Beneka A, et al. Defining the Traditional Mediterranean Lifestyle: Joint International Consensus Statement. Lifestyle Med [Internet]. 2024 Oct 1 [cited 2024 Oct 24];5(4):e115. Available from: https://onlinelibrary.wiley.com/doi/full/10.1002/lim2.115

RECIPE INDEX

Made in the USA
Las Vegas, NV
10 January 2025